laghman

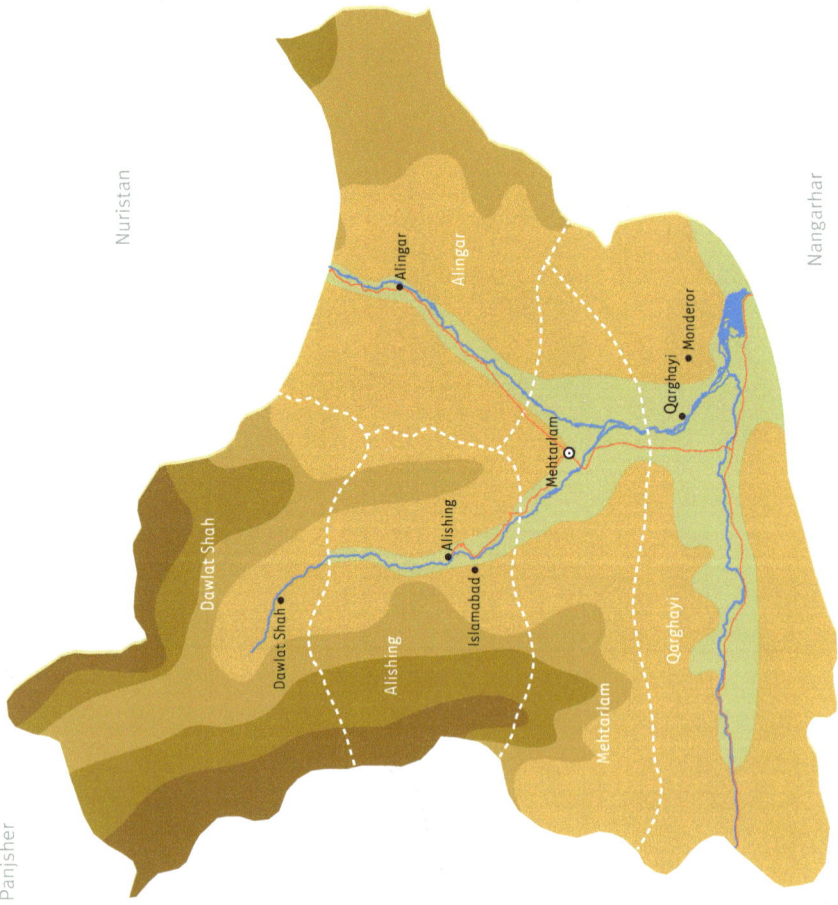

Laghman

Paved Road
District Border
River
Provincial Center
City

LOWER ELEVATION   HIGHER ELEVATION

Panjsher

Nuristan

Kunar

Kapisa

Dawlat Shah

Alishing

Dawlat Shah

Islamabad

Alishing

Alingar

Alingar

Mehtarlam

Mehtarlam

Qarghayi

Monderor

Qarghayi

Kabul

Nangarhar

Table of Contents

List of Tables and Maps

LIST OF TABLES

LIST OF MAPS

Acronyms and Key Terms

ABP	Afghan Border Police
ACNP	Afghan Counter Narcotics Police
ADP/E	Alternative Development Program for the Eastern Zone
ADT	Agribusiness Development Team
AICC	Afghanistan International Chamber of Commerce
AISA	Afghanistan Investment Services Association
ANA	Afghan National Army
ANP	Afghan National Police
AWCC	Afghan Wireless Communication Company
BEFA	Basic Education for Afghanistan
BHC	Basic Health Center
CA	Civil Affairs
CSTC-A	Combined Security Transition Command-Afghanistan
CDC	Community Development Council
CERP	Commander's Emergency Response Program
CHC	Comprehensive Health Center
CID	Criminal Investigation Division
COIN	Counter Insurgency
CSO	Central Statistics Office
DDS	District Development Shura
DIAG	Disbandment of Illegal Armed Groups
DoS	US Department of State
FATA	Federally Administered Tribal Areas
FOB	Forward Operating Base
GIRoA	Government of the Islamic Republic of Afghanistan
HIG or HIH	Hezb-e Islami Gulbuddin ("Islamic Party" formed by Gulbuddin Hekmatyar)
HIK	Hezb-e Islami Khalis ("Islamic Party" formed by Mohammad Yunus Khalis)
HP	Health Post
HTS	Human Terrain System
IARCSC	Independent Administrative Reform and Civil Service Commission

CRC	International Committee of the Red Cross
IDLG	Independent Directorate for Local Governance
IED	Improvised Explosive Device
IMC	International Medical Corps
IO	International Organization
IRoA	Islamic Republic of Afghanistan
ISAF	International Security Assistance Force
ISI	Inter-Services Intelligence (Pakistan)
Jamiatis or JI	Jamiat-e Islami ("Islamic Union")
LGCD	Local Governance Capacity Development Program
MADERA	Mission d'Aide Des Economies Rural Afghanistan
Meshrano Jirga	Elders' Assembly, upper house of Afghan National Assembly
MRRD	Ministry of Rural Rehabilitation and Development
MoE	Ministry of Education
MoI	Ministry of the Interior
MoPH	Ministry of Public Health
MoPW	Ministry of Public Works
Mustafiat	Department of Finance
NATO	North Atlantic Treaty Organization
NDS	National Directorate for Security
NGO	Non-Governmental Organization
NSP	National Solidarity Program
NWFP	North West Frontier Province
PAR	Public Administration Reform
PC	Provincial Council
PDC	Provincial Development Council
PRT	Provincial Reconstruction Team
RAH	Reconstruction Agency of Hindu Kush
SCA	Swedish Committee for Afghanistan
UN	United Nations
UNAMA	United Nations Assistance Mission in Afghanistan
UNOPS	United Nations Office for Project Services
USACE	US Army Corp of Engineers
USAID	US Agency for International Development
USDA	US Department of Agriculture
USG	United States Government
VOA	Voice of America
Wali	Governor
Wolesi Jirga	People's Assembly, lower house of Afghan National Assembly
Woluswal	District Administrator

Guide to the Handbook

This handbook is a concise field guide to Laghman for internationals deploying to the province. Field personnel have used these guides in Afghanistan since June 2008 to accelerate their orientation process and to serve as a refresher on different aspects of the province during their tour.

Reading this book will provide a basic understanding of the people, places, history, culture, politics, economy, needs, and ideas of Laghman. Building upon this understanding can help you:

- build rapport and a regular dialogue with local leaders,

- plan and implement pragmatic strategies (security, political, economic) to address sources of instability,

- influence communities to support the political process, not the insurgents, and

- build the capacity and legitimacy of a self-sufficient Afghan government and economy.

As you read the handbook and continue your inquiry in the province, seek to understand the influential leaders and groups in your local area and what beliefs and relationships drive their behavior. Think about the sources of violence in the area and whether groups are pursuing interests in a way that promotes conflict or stability. Finally, consider how various types of activities – key leader engagement, development assistance, security operations, security assistance, or public diplomacy – can effectively influence communities to work within the political process and oppose insurgency.

SOURCES AND METHODS

These handbooks are not intended as original academic research but as concise, readable summaries for practitioners in the field. The editorial team relies on its collective field experience and knowledge of the province, as well as key sources such as the official Islamic Republic of Afghanistan (IRoA), United Nations, and United States Government (USG) publications and those sources listed in the Appendix.

The editors made every effort to ensure accuracy. It should be noted, however, that there is often considerable disagreement regarding what is "ground truth" in Laghman, and things are constantly changing. As such, consider this book part of your orientation, and not an all-inclusive source for everything you need to know.

Information in this handbook is unclassified. The views and opinions expressed in this handbook are those of IDS International and in no way reflect the views of the United States Government or the United States Army.

THE ELECTRONIC UPDATE

Look for electronic updates to this book at *www.idsinternational.net/ afpakbooks*. Updates will cover any new developments, issues, and leaders that have emerged after publication. They will also provide corrections and expanded content in key areas based on feedback from readers.

We hope the handbook will continue to be a valuable tool in thinking about the challenges in Laghman. If you have questions, comments or feedback for future updates or editions please email *afpakbooks@idsinternational.net*.

ABOUT IDS INTERNATIONAL

Publisher of Afghanistan Provincial Handbook Series and the FATA/NWFP Pakistan Books

This book is one of a series of handbooks on Afghanistan provinces and regions of Pakistan. Titles include Ghazni, Helmand, Kandahar, Khost, Kunar, Laghman, Nangarhar, Nuristan, Paktya, and Paktika. Pakistan titles include NWFP and FATA. In addition to publishing these handbooks, IDS International provides training and analysis to government and private organizations in the areas of politics, economics, culture, stability operations, reconstruction, counterinsurgency, and interagency relations. In particular, IDS is a leading trainer of the US military in working with Provincial Reconstruction Teams (PRTs) in Iraq and Afghanistan. IDS offers its clients expertise and experience in the difficult work of interagency collaboration in complex operations. The writers and editors on this project offer a lifetime of experience working in these provinces and share a dedication to bringing peace and prosperity to the people of Afghanistan.

Authors: Chris Corsten, Dr. Ghulam Farouq Samim, and Michelle Parker
Editors: Nick Dowling and Tom Praster
Assistant Editors: Tom Viehe and Chris Hall

IDS INTERNATIONAL GOVERNMENT SERVICES

1916 Wilson Boulevard

Suite 302

Arlington, VA 22201

703-875-2212

www.idsinternational.net

afpakbooks@idsinternational.net

PUBLISHED: JUNE 2009

This and other AfPak handbooks may be bought in either hard copy, digital, or audiobook format. Samples are available upon request. IDS International is also a leading provider of training and support on the cultural, political, economic, interagency, and information aspects of conflict. Direct all inquires to *afpakbooks@idsinternational.net* or call 703-875-2212

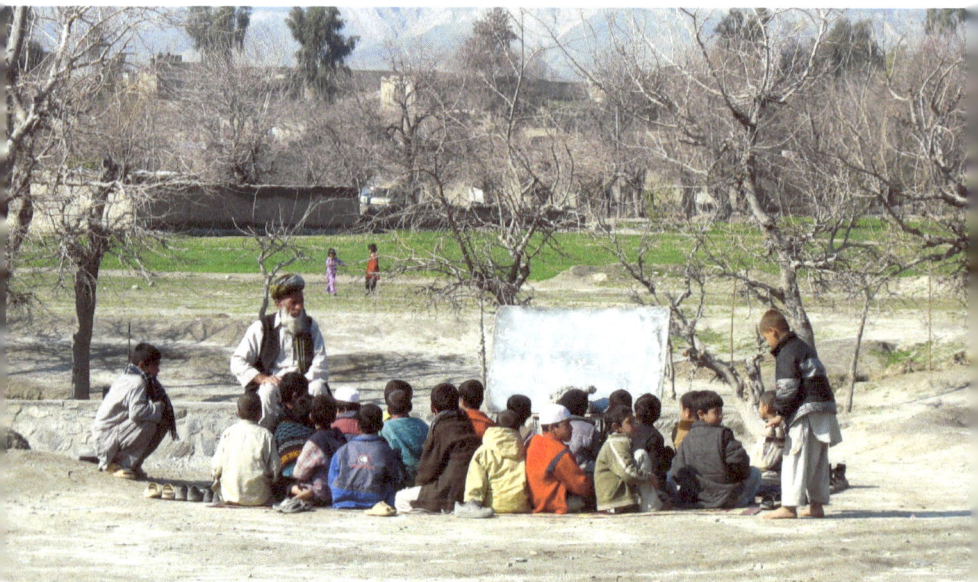

Laghmanis pride themselves on their education, which allows them to rise to high positions within the national government. Today, while education is still valued, many classes are held outdoors because schools are either overcrowded or lack buildings all together.

PHOTO BY AIR FORCE CAPT. GERARDO GONZALEZ

Chapter 1
Overview and Orientation

L aghman is a ruggedly beautiful province with a contrast of steep, unforgiving mountains and fertile river valleys. From the air, Laghman is easily distinguished by the giant green "Y" of forest carved into the sloping hills near the Alingar and Alishing rivers. The rivers meet in the provincial capital of Mehtarlam. Mehtarlam boasts a bustling market where traders sell small goods from Pakistan and China and farmers line the streets with carts of their recent harvests. Further south, the river flows into Qarghayi, feeding a very prosperous area of farms and orchards before emptying into the Kabul River. Throughout the province a rural population farms intricately terraced fields fed by a maze of irrigation canals.

Laghmani farmers grow a variety of fruits, vegetables, wheat, and rice. Laghman has been historically famous for its fruit orchards, most of which fell into disrepair during the decades of war and are just now starting to prosper again. Orchards of apricots, peaches, grapes, apples, and citrus fruits have been replanted, and the fruit is now being sold in markets and exported to other areas of the country. Laghman also contains small mines of precious stones such as emeralds, aquamarines, tourmalines, and rubies. The northern area of the province used to be full of trees, but the timber trade is taking its toll on these forests.

Laghman's main road systems have been in disrepair for decades. New road paving plans will link most of the province to the provincial center and the main markets of Jalalabad and Kabul. Still, the more secluded areas in the northwest have little road access and remain cut off from most of the province. The trails that run through these valleys are natural transit routes. Traffickers haul drugs through Laghman for processing in Nangarhar or for access to Afghanistan's northern border with Tajikistan. The mujahedin crossed Laghman with weapons and ammunition to fight against the Soviets. Today Laghman is still a transit route for insurgents and drugs.

Three large ethnic groups live in Laghman: Pashtuns, Tajiks, and Pashai. The people of Laghman speak both Pashto and Dari fluently, although their unusual Dari accent is sometimes ridiculed. Laghmanis are Sunni Muslims and are generally moderate in their religious beliefs. Before Islam, Laghman was home to both Hindus and Buddhists. Small communities of Hindus and Sikhs sold their land and property and fled Laghman during the civil war. There is still a small population of Sikhs near Mehtarlam. Laghman has a more learned and literate population than most other provinces, and Laghmanis have a reputation of being clever and savvy in professional dealings.

Most Laghmanis have been strong allies in the fight against the Taliban and al-Qaeda, and much of the province was stable by Afghan standards for several years after the start of Operation Enduring Freedom. However, the northern parts of the province – most notably Dawlat Shah, northern Alishing, and northern Alingar – were extremely dangerous environments. A few years ago the province began receiving more military and reconstruction attention – mostly road construction. The regional environment has progressed slowly through improved governance, the formation of a PRT, added maneuver forces, and significant assistance activities. The establishment of an observation post (OP) near Alishing has had a positive effect on security and the economy along the Alishing branch. As long as there is insurgent activity in the Eastern Region, however, Laghman's transit routes and remote regions will continue to be a focus of military attention. Most Laghmanis look forward to the day when they can return to simply tending their fields and livestock.

ORIENTATION

Laghman borders six other provinces: Nangarhar to the south, Kunar to the east, Nuristan to the northeast, Panjsher to the northwest, Kapisa to the west, and Kabul to the southwest. With valleys that connect most of these provinces to the rugged and remote mountain passes in the province, Laghman has historically been a preferred route of smugglers and outlaws.

The population in the north is settled along the two primary river valleys of Alingar and Dawlat Shah/Alishing, which meet in the capital, Mehtarlam, to form a "Y" shape. In the south, the population is scattered across the fertile plains of the Alingar and Kabul rivers. There is no industry to speak of and most of the farming is at a subsistence level. There are minimal job opportunities available in the province. Many Laghmanis work in Iran and Pakistan and send back remittances.

The province covers an area of 3,408 sq km. More than half of the province is mountainous or semi-mountainous terrain (55.4 percent), while around 40.9 percent of the area is made up of flatland.

Districts

Laghman has only five districts, three of which are mountainous: Dawlat Shah, Alishing, and Alingar. Alingar and Alishing possess some of the last remaining forests in Afghanistan, filled with many different kinds of trees, such as pine (which produces pine nuts for export), *baloot* (used for firewood), wild olive trees, and *nashtar* (used as timber). The remaining two districts, Mehtarlam and Qarghayi, have plains used for agriculture. The western third of the Mehtarlam district is relatively inaccessible, with terrain resembling the badlands of South Dakota.

Key Towns

Mehtarlam is the only major town in Laghman. The outlying districts each have a district center with a market and district-level offices but offer little else.

Mehtarlam is the provincial capital with a population of about 113,000, which is small compared to other provincial capitals. Mehtarlam is linked with the main Kabul-Jalalabad highway through an 18-km stretch of paved road, providing it with easy access to the rest of the country. The city is linked to nearly all major population centers in Laghman by paved roads. The exception is the road to Dawlat Shah, which is currently under construction. Located at the confluence of the Alingar and Alishing Rivers, Mehtarlam is the main market for not only Laghman but also the western and central valleys of Nuristan. The city is home to an ancient and beautiful garden called Bagh-e Qala-e Saraj that was built by King Habibullah Khan at the beginning of the 20th century. The large mosque in town is called Jame Jomat.

Table 1. District Populations

DISTRICT	CENTER	POPULATION	TRIBES, ETHNICITIES
Alingar	Alingar	82,483	Pashtun Mixed, Pashai, Tajik
Alishing	Alishing	69,595	Pashtun Mixed, Pashai, Tajik
Dawlat Shah	Dawlat Shah	35,610	Pashai, Tajik, Kata, Hazara, Panshiri, Mixed Pashtun
Mehtarlam	Mehtarlam	135,075	Mixed
Qarghayi	Qarghayi	126,439	Pashtun Mixed
Total		**449,202**	

RELEVANT HISTORICAL ISSUES

From Ancient to Modern Times

During the invasion of Alexander the Great, this region was known as Lampaka. In the seventh century, the Chinese traveler Xuan Zang visited the area and noted that it was settled mostly by Hindus and a few Buddhists. By the end of the first millennium, Sultan Mahmud Ghaznawi reportedly battled a these people as he was spreading Islam throughout the region. The battle gave the region its name, Lakman, meaning 100,000 men. Ancient inscriptions found in Laghman, now in the Kabul Museum, show that the passes in the province were on the major trading route between India and Palmyra, in present-day Syria. Indeed, a section of the Kabul-Mehtarlam highway is called Tangi Abrishom, which means Narrow Way of Silk. Laghman became a province during

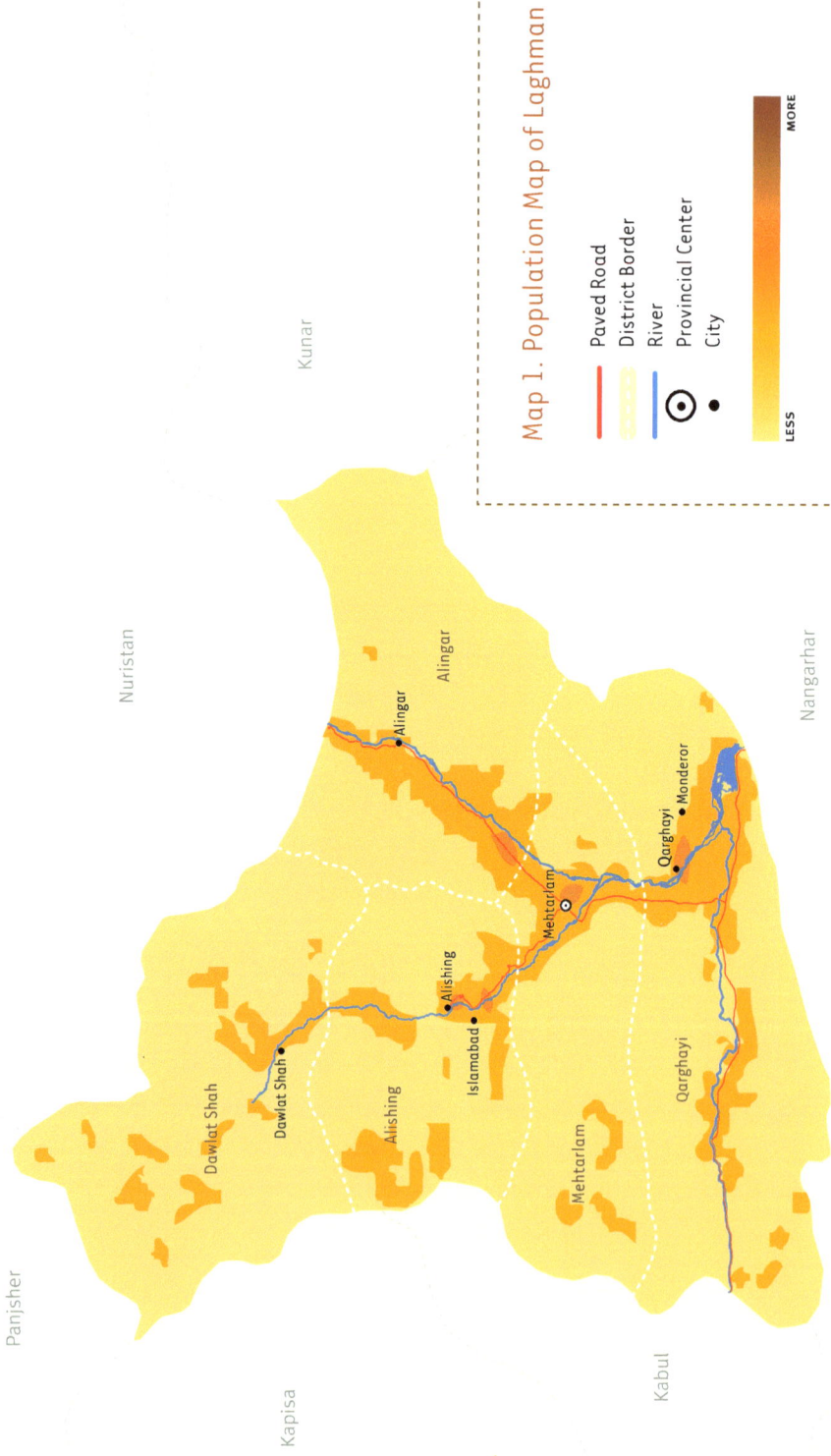

Map 1. Population Map of Laghman

Paved Road		
District Border		
River		
Provincial Center		
City		

LESS — MORE

the rule of King Zahir Shah, and its current boundaries were set during the communist regime of the 1980s. Due to its lack of resources and arable land, many Laghmanis focused on education prior to the Soviet invasion in 1978. This was a major source of pride for Laghmanis as they rose to high positions in the national government. Laghmanis also have a history of staunch anti-communism, staging protests and challenging the former communist regimes.

Communist Era (1978-1992)

Laghmanis were instrumental in the fight against the Soviet Union's occupation. The Islamic movement in Laghman was greatly influenced by Ikhwanul Muslimeen of the Islamic Brotherhood in Egypt, and many Islamic leaders were staunch followers of his concepts. After a failed coup against Sardar Daoud Khan's regime, some of the members from the Islamic movement, including Gulbuddin Hekmatyar and Burhanuddin Rabbani, took refuge in Pakistan and stayed there under the direct support of Pakistan's Inter-Services Intelligence (ISI) until the Soviet invasion of Afghanistan.

In Pakistan, many Afghan refugees divided themselves between these two groups: Jamiat-e Islami ("Islamic Union," also known as Jamiatis or JI) under Rabbani and Hezb-e Islami ("Islamic Party," also known as Hezbis or HIG) under Hekmatyar. Jamiat-e Islami consisted mostly of intellectuals; Hezb-e Islami contained mostly young and emotional jihadists. Other small factions existed but played very minor roles. The factions not only fought the Soviets, but also turned on each other.

The communist era was also noteworthy for the Soviet land distribution policies, which took land from chieftains and redistributed it among farmers. These policies led to significant land disputes for years to come, which created more jihadis.

Table 2. Siginficant Jihadi Actors

NAME	ORGANZIATION	DISTRICT
Malem Abdullah Jan	Hezb-e Islami Gulbuddin	Dawlat Shah
Engineer Alim Qarar	Hezb-e Islami Gulbuddin	Alingar
Naser Mansoor	Hezb-e Islami Gulbuddin	Mehtarlam
Dai Gul	Jamiat-e Islami	Dawlat Shah
Tareq	Jamiat-e Islami	Dawlat Shah
Dr. Abdullah Laghmani	Jamiat-e Islami	Mehtarlam
Commander Khaled	Jamiat-e Islami	Dawlat Shah
Malawi Farashghan	Haratkat-e Enqelabe Islami	Dawlat Shah
Dawlat Shah	Ittehad-e Islami Party	N/A

Mujahedin and Taliban Era (1992-2001)

The mujahedin era was very hard on the Laghmani people due to clashes between rival factions of the former mujahedin. HIG dominated the province politically, but the group was not unified. As a result, power struggles between the mujahedin-era governor Abdullah Wahidi, Engineer Qarar, and Naser Mansoor led to violence. The rivalries were fierce, as evidenced when Engineer Qarar murdered Mansoor.

In 1996, the population welcomed the Taliban, viewing them as a stable alternative to the mujahedin's bloodshed. Most HIG commanders retreated to Pakistan during the Taliban takeover. The Laghmanis often joke that a single jeep with a gunner and loudspeaker shouting "Allahu

Akbar!" took Laghman. Such a description is not far from the truth. Only 100 Taliban were posted to the province, but they kept order by strictly enforcing sharia and torturing people to collect information about illegal arms caches and insurgents. During this era, former governor Abdullah Wahidi was murdered in a blood feud.

Contemporary Events (2001-Present)

As coalition forces defeated the Taliban in the north, former warlords took advantage of the situation and rushed into Laghman to disarm the Taliban. Engineer Qarar, who had joined the Taliban late, changed sides again and was one of the first on the scene, with the goal of securing power. Despite having previously murdered Mansoor, he was elected to the lower house of parliament and presently serves as a Laghmani MP. A number of Jamiat-e Islami warlords returned, including Esmatullah Mohabat, who was notorious for seeking refuge with the Northern Alliance commander, Ahmad Shah Massoud, after killing members of his own family in Laghman. He was also elected to the lower house of parliament, but soon after was murdered in a dispute with a local merchant, Haji Sardar. Abdul Hadi Wahidi, the former governor's brother, now holds that seat. The other JI warlord to return was Dr. Abdullah Laghmani, who currently serves as the deputy director of Afghanistan's National Directorate for Security (NDS) in Kabul.

Since 2001, Laghman has had five governors. The first was Abdul Hadi Wahidi, whose brother held the post years before. Next was Ibrahim Babakarkhel from the National Liberation Front. Third was Shah Mahmood Safi. All three of these governors were considered exceptionally weak and could not combat the power of the warlords. Gulab Mangal assumed the governorship in 2006 and was considered one of the most effective governors in Afghanistan. Laghmanis respected his leadership and ability to contain the warlords. The population credited him with paving key roads in Alishing and Alingar valleys, even though one road was already under construction upon his arrival and the US military determined that the other was strategically important for security. Due to his ability and reputation, he was moved to the more volatile Helmand in March 2008. The current governor is Lutfullah Mashal, a former spokesmen of the Ministry of Interior and a reporter for the Christian Science Monitor.

In 2008 and 2009, the Taliban threat worsened due to a lack of government influence in the more volatile areas of Dawlat Shah and Alishing. Civilian deaths during US operations also helped to catalyze the threat, like those in Galouch and Masamut-e Bala. Although US forces have tried to make reparations for these attacks, a rift still remains between the affected population and the military. At the same time, the more central areas of Laghman have flourished due to their relative stability and access to markets. Laghman remains one of the safest provinces in the Eastern Region.

One area in which the military has excelled is road building. Commander's Emergency Response Program (CERP) funds have financed building the main road systems linking the districts to the capital, as well as the main highway between Kabul and the Pakistan border. The building of the hardball road from Mehtarlam to Alishing and the establishment of an observation post (OP) near Alishing has had a positive effect on both security and the economy along the Alishing branch. The PRT hopes to expand this success by extending the hardball road northwest to Dawlat Shah. Still, the insurgents are able to exert their influence in the small valleys off the main roads, which are less accessible to the police and other government agencies. Laghman is not as populated as Nangarhar and does not have nearly the same level of insurgents as Kunar. Therefore, Laghman is often seen as a lower priority for US donors and military funding.

A renewed development surge aims to strengthen stability in the central areas and bring the outlying districts under greater government influence. Although significant progress has been made on road systems, other sectors need attention as well. Irrigation systems in Laghman are in disrepair, a large number of schools need to be built, and reliable power is non-existent. With the addition of new funds coming to the PRTs, the military will be able to work with the Afghan government and local authorities on a surge of projects in each sector to permanently fix many of the problems at the same time. Insurgents are increasing information campaigns, especially in areas that have little access to the rest of the province.

Divisions that formed between different mujahedin commanders over the past thirty years continue to plague the province today. The deaths of Esmatullah Mohabat and Abdullah Wahidi left two men – Engineer Qarar (MP for Laghman) and Dr. Abdullah (deputy director of NDS) vying for power and influence in Laghman. Qarar's murder of Naser Mansoor caused many of Mansoor's HIG sub-commanders to align with Jamiat-e Islami's Dr. Abdullah. Haji Sardar is currently in jail for the murder of Esmatullah Mohabat, but rumors swirled that Hazrat Ali, former warlord turned MP in Nangarhar, was also involved.

A tribal shura gathers to discuss local matters. Tribes are the most powerful structure in Pashtun society. Working to resolve conflict through consensus, shuras are set up to redress wrongs and address issues of pride.

PHOTO BY CAPT WALTER CHRISTIAN

Chapter 2
Ethnicity, Tribes,
Languages, and Religion

ETHNICITY

The major ethnic groups living in Laghman province, from largest to smallest, are Pashtuns, Pashai, and Tajiks. There are a few Nuristani families living in Alingar and Dawlat Shah, and nomadic Kuchi come to Laghman during the winter months.

Table 3. Ethnicity by District

DISTRICT	PASHTUN	TAJIK	PASHAI
Alingar	70%	5%	25%
Alishing	25%	15%	60%
Dawlat Shah	1%	29%	70%
Mehtarlam	60%	35%	5%
Qarghayi	60%	20%	20%

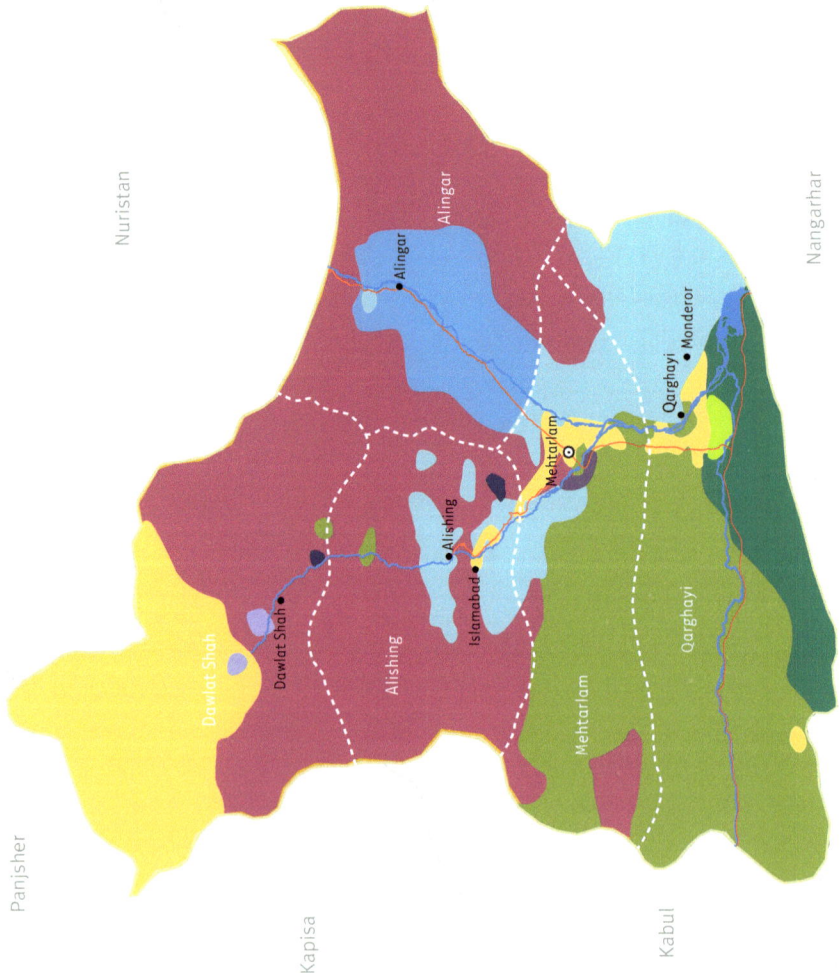

Map 2. Tribal Map of Laghman

——	Paved Road
	District Border
	River
⊙	Provincial Center
•	City
	Tajik
	Pashai
	Kata Nuristani
	Kuchi Pashtun
	Safi Pashtun
	Wardak Pashtun
	Abdulrahimzail Ghilzai Pashtun
	Naser Ghilzai Pashtun
	Niazi Ghilzai Pashtun
	Mixed Ghilzai Pashtun

Kunar

Nuristan

Nangarhar

Panjsher

Kapisa

Kabul

Alingar

Alingar

Alishing

Alishing

Islamabad

Dawlat Shah

Dawlat Shah

Alishing

Mehtarlam

Mehtarlam

Qarghayi

Qarghayi

Monderor

Pashtun

Pashtuns are the largest ethnic group in Laghman, with 11 Pashtun tribes making up 51 percent of the population. They own most of the arable land in Laghman, located on both sides of the Alishing and Alingar Rivers and in Qarghayi. Most make their living from agriculture. Pashtun tribes in Laghman generally get along with each other quite well, as shown by the peacefulness of Qarghayi, where many different Pashtun tribes reside. Pashtun tribes are mixed together in such a way that boundaries cannot be drawn and rivalries and power struggles between tribes are rare. The tribes are listed by district in Table 4.

Table 4. Pashtun Tribes of Laghman

DISTRICT	TRIBES
Alingar	Niazi and Aloko/Alokazai, Safi
Alishing	Safi, Amarkhel, Tarakhel, Jabarkhel, and other small tribes
Dawlat Shah	Kuchi
Mehtarlam	Sahak, Safi, Babarkarhel, Hossainkhel, Kaker, Mosahkel, Tarakhel, Wardak, Omarkhel, and other small tribes
Qarghayi	Abdulrahimzail, Hodkhel, Naser, Kharoti, Jabarkhel, Ibrahimkhel, Farmankhel, Oriakhel, Tarakhel, and other small tribes

Pashai

The Pashai make up the second largest ethnic group in Laghman. They are located primarily in Dawlat Shah, Alingar, and parts of Alishing districts. Pashai inhabit northern Nangarhar, Laghman, and parts of Nuristan. Their native tongue is a Dardic language, a language group that extends to the foothills of the Hindu Kush from Afghanistan to India. They are also referred to as Kohistani, a term describing people who live in the mountains. They are occasionally referred to as *Shurrhi*, a derisive term for "hillbilly." They typically do not ally with any Pashtuns.

Tajik

Tajiks primarily speak Dari, the Afghan version of Farsi, and in Laghman are all Sunni Muslims. Tajiks are the third largest ethnicity in Laghman. Alone, Tajiks make up 22 percent of the population in Laghman, and although comprised of different tribes, are often brought together by the perceived common threat posed by Pashtuns. Most Tajik areas of Laghman are from mixed tribal families.

Kuchi

The Kuchi are a migratory ethnic group who travel throughout Afghanistan. In winter four percent of the overall Kuchi population stay in Laghman, living in 40 communities. Of these communities, two percent are short-range migratory, one percent are settled, and 97 percent are long-range migratory. Due to migration, there are almost no Kuchi in Laghman during the summer.

TRIBES

The tribe is the most powerful structure of Pashtun society and provides an informal governance structure. Most of the other ethnicities in Laghman embrace a Pashtun-like tribal structure, using the same mechanisms to self-govern. Since Afghanistan has never had a strong central government, tribes are essential to survival, livelihood, and identity. Tribal elders are called *maliks*, and are appointed by the community based upon their ability to lead and bring resources to the tribe. The maliks resolve conflict, allocate justice, make decisions on behalf of the tribe, and represent tribal interests to external parties such as the central government or the US military.

Tribal society works on a group decision-making structure rather than an individual decision-making structure. All decisions for the tribe or subsections within a tribe are determined through consensus. The goal of justice is to promote group harmony rather than punish an individual.

There are two primary mechanisms for tribal elders to make decisions. The first is called a *jirga*, which is a meeting held to make a specific decision. It can involve people from within or outside of the tribe. Any decision made in a jirga is considered binding.

The other meeting type is called a *shura*, from the Arabic word for consultation. Shuras seek to redress wrongs through arbitration, and address issues of pride and reparations more than they actually impose punishment. Shuras have become more militarized in Afghanistan after decades of war, acting as short-term advisory councils that can include elders, commanders, and landowners.

LANGUAGES

Pashto, Dari, and Pashai are the three main languages spoken in Laghman. Pashto is the most common because it is the primary language of the largest ethnic group in the province, and most Laghmanis are able to speak it. Tajiks speak Dari as their first language, and Pashto as their second. Most Pashai speakers also speak Pashto or Dari, but they may speak only Pashai in remote villages. Pashai interpreters are rare but are very important, especially for operating in the Mayl, Gonapaland, and northern Alishing valley areas. English is being taught in some schools, and some elders may speak Russian.

THE ROLE OF RELIGION

Islam is very important to the culture of most Afghans in Laghman. Even if a person is not truly pious he will at least appear to be, and it would be unwise to challenge that. No outsider should ever speak poorly about Islam or accuse an Afghan of being un-Islamic. It is good to compliment someone for being a good Muslim, but the topic of religion should be approached lightly, if at all.

Mullahs have a special place of influence over the people. Since Afghanistan is an Islamic republic, there is no separation between religion and government. Any law made must be in line with Islamic principles for it to be accepted. The Director of Religious Affairs (often called Director of Haj) is the government's official representative for the mullah community in the province. He has significant influence over the mullahs throughout the districts and is considered the "mouthpiece" of the mullah community.

A network of mullahs is run through the director's office in Mehtarlam. Each district has several mullahs that often come to Mehtarlam to represent the mosques and communities of their districts. The current director is quite weak and does not have much influence over the other mullahs in the districts. However, the Ulema Shura, made up of three to four of the most influential mullahs in the province, has been a good organization for the military to engage in order to influence the mullahs in the districts and get messages out through Friday prayers. Consistent engagements with the mullah community through the Ulema Shura are one of the best ways to win the support of the community. Mullahs who support and speak in favor of the international community and US military are one of the keys to support from the local population.

RELEVANT CULTURAL POINTS

Afghans are a very proud people. Although they are accepting to outsiders when it benefits them, there is always a feeling of mistrust. Throughout recent history, many conquering armies and unstable governments have come and gone, always promising stability, security, and economic development. Very few of these promises have been kept. Corruption and a "me first" mentality has loomed as stability has decreased. Afghans do not appreciate a person raising their voice and openly fighting or swearing. It is rare to see two Afghans yelling at each other for an extended time during meetings. Normally, when an Afghan wants to make a strong point, he will raise his voice and not be challenged by anyone else raising his voice in return. Patience is important when meeting with Afghans. Consensus is important when meeting with a shura, and everyone needs a chance to speak. Often meetings will end with no resolution, and this is often fine with Afghans.

Respect and honor are very important to Afghans. Always act respectfully by shaking hands with everyone when you enter a room. Even when a group is already meeting, it is customary for new arrivals to interrupt the meeting to shake hands with everyone. This is not considered rude by Afghans, but normal. When shaking hands with someone, always use the right hand and then place your hand directly on your heart as a sign of respect. If you are able to, take off your shoes when entering a room when you see that others have done this. Normally, the host will tell you not to take them off, but it is polite to offer.

Attorneys from Laghman listen to a lecture during a legal seminar. While Governor Mashal is thought to have performed well in his first 12 months in office, rule of law still remains weak in the province. The seminar was set up to better prepare attorneys to practice law in their districts.

PHOTO BY STAFF SGT. DAVID HOPKINS

Chapter 3
Government and Leadership

Laghman is one of the more stable provinces in the Eastern Region and has seen some growth in governance capacity and economic activity. Many credit former governor Mangal and, to a lesser degree, the current governor Lutfallah Mashal. Governor Mashal faces twin challenges of sustaining popular support for the government and managing the residual mujahedin political rivalries in the leading political groups.

HOW THE GOVERNMENT OFFICIALLY WORKS

Central Control

Authority and power in Afghanistan are concentrated in the national government as a means to counter the power of warlords in the provinces. As such, the provincial government is limited to an advisory role for the central government, while decisions on everything from policy to funding priorities are made in Kabul.

Provincial Government

A governor (*wali*) heads the provincial government and reports to the Independent Directorate for Local Governance (IDLG), located in the Executive Office of the President. A deputy and several staff that oversee provincial government management assist him.

Ministries in Kabul execute their policies and programs through departments located at the provincial level. Ministers, with the approval of the president, appoint provincial directors who manage the departments. The director reports to and receives funds from the ministry in Kabul. The governor does not have budgetary authority over any of these departments, but must approve all expenditures before they are processed by the Department of Finance (*Mustafiat*).

The Provincial Council (PC), an elected body at the provincial level, provides a voice for the people in advising on provincial issues. The PC reports directly to the president and has no budget. Its relevance is largely dependent on the governor's support and on its members' individual resources and ambition.

The Provincial Development Committee (PDC), including the governor and department heads, is responsible for creating the Provincial Development Plan (PDP) and coordinating with key players on development needs. External players such as the UN, PRT, and interested NGOs also attend meetings.

District and Local Governance

Government at the district level mirrors the provincial government with the *woluswal* (district administrator or sub-governor), police chief, National Directorate of Security officer, clerks, and a small police force. Ministry sub-departments also operate at the district level, but are not present in every district. In 2007, District Development Assemblies (DDA) were formed in order to plan, prioritize, and coordinate development activities at the district level. Below the district level, the only formal governance structures are the Community Development Councils (CDCs). The CDCs help the Ministry of Rural Rehabilitation and Development (MRRD) manage the National Solidarity Program.

The municipality of Mehtarlam is led by a mayor appointed by the IDLG, in consultation with the governor. Municipalities are independent from the provincial government; they are free to plan, fund, and implement projects, and can tax local businesses.

HOW IT ACTUALLY WORKS

Provincial Government

Governor Mashal is well educated and a strong ally of President Karzai but has received mixed reviews on his performance thus far. He is credited with working closely with the PRT and other donors to bring development to Laghman and is looking forward with larger development plans. Government officials are coordinating efforts well with local elders, creating a better sense of community. This has gained the governor some popularity in the province. However, security and rule of law are still major stumbling blocks due to rumors of corruption and lack of real justice.

Provincial Council

The Provincial Council (PC) in Laghman has nine members, three of whom are female. The PC is very active and brings a full agenda to every weekly meeting. PC members work closely with Governor Mashal and the PRT on development, economic, and security issues. PC meetings are always well attended, and PC members represent the interests of Laghmanis well. The PC mainly focuses on helping the local population mediate disputes within their own communities because they feel the justice system in Laghman is too corrupt to use effectively. In April 2008, PC member Gulzar Sangarwal from Alingar was arrested by NDS for alleged ties with insurgents. The other members of the PC protested his arrest, and he was released with the intervention of a Laghmani MP. In May, the NDS chief who arrested him was removed from his position.

The PC is the only body of officials at the provincial level that is elected from the local population. It is important to coordinate with the PC on major issues, as this raises their clout, can help influence the population, and brings confidence in the democratic process.

District and Local-level Government

There is still a great challenge involved with planning at a district level because so many valleys are isolated and thus unconcerned with affairs in the next valley over. The government set up District Development Assemblies (DDA) as part of the local development plan, but they have not accomplished much to date.

In Afghanistan, traditional organizations based on tribe, culture, and religion continue to be the most legitimate and effective bodies available on a local level. The dynamics are shifting as the provincial government reaches out to elders and mullahs. Some traditional leaders are being incorporated into the official government, but others are resisting these overtures.

These informal bodies dispense justice, mediate conflicts, and can even raise militias (*arbakai*) if they feel threatened. The key decision-makers can be a group consisting of any combination of the following: tribal elder (*malik*), land owner (*khan*), religious Lleader (*mullah*), and water manager (*mirab*). The types of issues resolved at this level include small legal disputes such as land disputes, small fights, petty theft, etc. The community will be the first to try to solve significant legal issue such as murder, large land disputes, or organized crime. If they cannot, they will refer the cases to the formal legal system.

SECURITY FORCES

Afghan National Army (ANA): The ANA remains the most trusted and capable security agency in Afghanistan, and the troops are not afraid to fight for their country. The troops have mentors from the US military and are receiving better equipment and training than before. There are two large ANA bases in Laghman. The first is adjacent to the PRT in Alikhel village of Mehtarlam. The second is stationed just north of Qaleh Najil village of Alishing. According to new information from the MoD, some ANA forces are also in Dawlat Shah and Kala Gush on the Laghman/Nuristan border. These forces operate under the corps command of Silab (201) in Jalalabad. With consistent training, the ANA will eventually be able to take over full security roles in Afghanistan.

National Directorate of Security (NDS): The Afghan intelligence service, NDS, is made up of highly educated officers. They are not trusted by the local population, but they have thwarted several terrorist attempts. As Dr. Abdullah is deputy director for NDS in Kabul, he uses this as a powerbase to assert his own authority in the province.

Afghan National Police (ANP): The ANP is not very strong in most of Laghman. They have virtually no presence in Dawlat Shah, minimal presence in Alishing and Alingar, but seem to be doing well in Qarghayi and Mehtarlam. General Omaryar has greatly improved the leadership of the ANP since taking over as Provincial Police Chief in October 2006. General Omaryar reports to the Ministry of the Interior. The police, due in large part to their very low pay, have been corrupt almost by necessity and therefore have a very poor reputation among the general populace. Training, equipment, and mentoring programs are gradually improving the capacity of the ANP, but behavior is an area that needs continual work.

POLITICAL PARTIES AND ELECTIONS

Hezb-e Islami (Gulbuddin Hekmatyar): The party was originally set up by Engineer Ibrahim Niazi as an Islamic student movement in the late 1970s at Kabul University. Later, Hekmatyar reestablished the party prior to the Soviet invasion as a voice against the communist regime. After the Soviet invasion, HIG became a powerful political-military entity in Afghanistan by partnering with Pakistan's Directorate of Inter-Services Intelligence (ISI). Two former HIG commanders in Laghman are prominent in the current government: Abdul Hadi Wahidi (MP) and Engineer Qarar (MP). HIG has actively opposed the Karzai administration since its inception and claims it is a puppet of the US. The organization continues to target government workers and buildings and supply routes for the counterinsurgents. HIG is considered a militant group and not a political party. However, Hezb-e Islami is a registered legal party in Afghanistan and claims to have no affiliation with Hekmatyar.

Jamiat-e Islami: Jamiat is one of the two largest political parties in Laghman and has an intense rivalry with HIG. Isamatullah Mohabat, who was killed after the parliamentary election, was a Jamiat member. Dr. Abdullah, the deputy director of NDS in Kabul, is also a prominent member who has influence in Laghman today. Many members of this party are working in the central government and several provincial governments. Because of the rivalry between JI and HIG, many members of HIG are being prevented from taking an active role in the government.

Hezb-e Afghan Millat (Afghan Nation Party): This is a national Pashtun party led by Finance Minister Dr. Anwar Ul-haq Ahadi. Its platform is based on unity, security, and creating an Islamic version of democracy. It maintains a muted, ethno-nationalist rhetoric. There are some members of this party in Laghman, but the party has only a very minor impact.

Ittehad-e Islami: This party has some members in Laghman, but it is not very influential. The one exception is Mawlawi Sayed Ulrahman, an Ittehad member who received the highest number of votes in the province for the lower house of the parliament (Wolesi Jirga). It is made up of former members of the Jamiat-e Islami party.

Laghman had 230,948 registered voters in the previous election and will most likely add more as the August 2009 election gets closer. The province has four lower house seats, one of which was reserved for a woman, and two upper house seats chosen by President Karzai. The Provincial Council has nine seats, with three reserved for women.

2009 ELECTIONS

Presidential and Provincial Council elections are scheduled to take place on 20 August 2009. When President Karzai's term expired in May, he began serving as a caretaker president until elections could be held. Candidates for president filed in May, but few national contenders emerged, as President Karzai persuaded many of his rivals not to challenge him. In terms of security, Afghan National Security Forces will be extensively involved in the elections, recruiting 23,000 police and soldiers for the event. The security of the elections represents a potential key moment for the summer fighting season between Taliban and Afghan/ Coalition forces. After the elections, changes in the Afghan government will include new senior appointments, including new ministers and governors. Late 2009 and 2010 will be a key period for these new officials to leverage their public mandate and expanded international assistance to deliver more accountable and credible governance to the Afghan people.

With elections looming, the rivalry between HIG and JI is expected to intensify as both seek to get their favored candidates elected to the PC. At the time of writing (June 2009), there has been little noticeable posturing between the two parties, but it could still be happening. Since Governor Mashal is a strong supporter of President Karzai, if Karzai loses the election, Mashal may be replaced with a new governor with ties to the new president.

A more detailed update on elections is included in the back folder of your book or can be downloaded at *www.idsinternational.net/afpakbooks*. The pre-elections update goes into the elections process in greater detail, and the post-election update summarizes the results and implications.

Table 5. Provincial Line Directors and Other Government Officials

NAME	POSITION	CONTACT NUMBER
Lutfullah Mashal	Governor	
Alhaaj Murtaza Hedayat Qalanderzia	Deputy Governor	0799-004-965
Abdul Mateen Aukhunzadah	Court Director	0700-589-121
Mohammad Afaq Baryalia	Executive Director	0797-181-648
Teacher Tor-Gul Arfan	Governor's Chief of Staff	0799-874-458
Muhibullah Lodeen	Sectorial Services Director	0799-137-328
Sayeed Ahmad Safi	Governor's Spokesman	0700-603-070
Brigadier General Abdul Karim Omaryar	Police Chief	0700-038-827
Colonel Sadullah	National Security Director	0799-343-583

NAME	POSITION	CONTACT NUMBER
Sayeed Jamaludeen Husnee	Education Director	0799-352-562
Dr. Abdul Majeed Mayrani	Work and Social Affairs Director	0700-642-186
Colonel Mohammad Jaan	ANA Commander	0774-413-529
Sayeed Anber Pacha	Appeals Court Director	0799-811-876
Mohammad Mihdi	Chief of Revenue Office	0700-486-390
Moulay Obaidullah	Judicial Director	0799-151-766
Mohammad Jafer	RRD Director	0700-642-426
Mohammad Ismail	Agriculture Director	0700-603-970
Eng. Mohammad Kazim	Refugee Director	0799-884-420
Dr. Abdul Ghafar	Red Crescent	0799-273-278
Lt Colonel Noor Badshah	Recruitment Commander	0799-246-232
Naqeebullah	Frontier Line Director (Border)	0799-534-944
Eng. Sayeed Abdul Rahim	Water Management Director	0799-829-835
Alhaaj-Muhibullah	Radio & TV Director	0700-161-885
Khalil-U-L-Rahman	Military Prosecution Director	0700-585-409
Hanifah	Women's Affairs Director	0700-586-433
Eng. Sayeed Nasir	Communication Director	0700-614-373
Moulay Safiullah	Religious Affairs Director	0799-196-442

NAME	POSITION	CONTACT NUMBER
Eng. Mohamaad Agha	Economic Director	0799-841-528
Ali Ahmad	Nomad Affairs Director	0799-692-486
Alhaaj-Mohammad Omer	Statistics Services Director	0799-660-384
Ahmad Husain	Transportation Director	0799-619-074
Eng. Mohammad Akram	Director of Irrigation	0799-836-599
Eng. Paindah Mohammad	Environmental Affairs Director	0700-188-773
Brigadier General Daoulat Mohammad	Prison Director	0700-210-168
Sayeed Agha	PCC Commander	0799-862-762
Farid Shah	DIAG Provincial Advisor	0700-005-697
Mohammad Shareef	Power and Energy Director	0799-442-897
Alhaj-Sayeed Wali	Sustenance Manager	0799-870-904
Eng. Abdul Mateen	Urban Development Representative	0799-286-601
Mohammad Sohail	Public Work Director	0799-498-298
Mihrabuldeen	Bank Manager	0700-031-725
Naseer Ahmad	Deputy Governor's Secretary	0700-064-500
Qari Mohammad Zubair	Governor's Office IT	0700-854-585
Mohammad Afzal	Governor's Office Meetings Director	0700-854-596

Table 6. Laghman District Sub- Governors

NAME	DISTRICT NAME	CONTACT NUMBER
Haji Alafshah Khan	Alingar	0799-524-466
Mohammad Qasim	Alishing	0772-650-231
Mohammad Arif	Qarghayi	0799-286-865
Haji Sardar Agha	Dawlat Shat	0773-949-725

Mehtarlam is run out of the governor's office; there is no sub-governor

LEADER PROFILES

Government/Political Leaders

Governor Lutfullah Mashal: Mashal, a Pashtun born in Paktya province, has been governor since March 2008, when he replaced Mohammad Mangal. Mashal is only 36 years old, Western-educated, and fluent in English. Mashal is strongly pro-Karzai and served in national and executive levels of the government. Prior to government service, Mashal was a linguist for Ambassador Khalilzad and a columnist for the Christian Science Monitor. He works closely with PRT officers on long-term planning for Laghman's agricultural development and economic growth with a focus on roads, power distribution, and watershed management. Mashal is credited with reducing insurgent attacks and roadside bombs as well as improving coordination between Laghman and Kabul. His main challenges involve trying to settle disputes between HIG and JI, rival parties that are fighting for influence in Laghman. Mashal has done a good job in his first 12 months in office, but governance, especially rule of law, must improve. Rumors persist that he receives bribes from contractors as "permission" to work in Laghman. In spite of these rumors, he is popular and Laghmanis support him. Mashal is very effective at using the media and recently staged several large demonstrations throughout Laghman protesting acts committed by insurgents. Mashal must instill confidence in citizens to look to their government and not insurgents. His continued focus should be rebuilding the Laghman infrastructure, providing economic opportunity, and establishing government legitimacy. Expect Mashal to assume a position of greater importance if Karzai wins re-election, but be replaced if Karzai loses.

Abdul Karim Omaryar, Chief of Police: Abdul Karim Omaryar was appointed chief of police in September 2006. Omaryar was a member of HIG during the mujahedin era. He later fought alongside the Northern Alliance against the Taliban. He served as the chief of police in neighboring Kapisa province before his posting in Laghman. He has a good relationship with Governor Mashal. The population supports Omaryar, and he is considered more professional and effective than previous police chiefs. He is credited with improving security in Qarghayi and Mehtarlam, but he has little influence in the more insecure areas of Dawlat Shah and Alishing.

Other Key Figures

Dr. Abdullah: Abdullah is the deputy director of the NDS and now resides in Kabul. He is one of the three most powerful people in Laghman. He was a low-level Jamiat-e Islami commander during the jihad against the Soviets and became close to the Northern Alliance led by Ahmad Shah Massoud and Marshal Qasim Fahim. Laghman was a stronghold of HIG before the Taliban, but after the Taliban left, Ismatullah Mohabat and Dr. Abdullah took control of most of the province. Former commanders of HIG operating under Naser Mansoor joined Abdullah after Naser was killed by Engineer Qarar in Alingar district.

Engineer Mohammad Alam Qarar: Qarar is from Alingar district but fled to Pakistan during the Soviet invasion. He became an influential HIG commander, fighting the Soviets in Alingar. He also fought against mujahedin rivals and is blamed for murdering his HIG rival, Mansoor. He is a political opportunist and a survivor. Qarar originally fought against the Taliban and then joined them later when it seemed that they could not be defeated. After the US invasion in 2001, Qarar quickly took advantage of the situation and switched sides in order to secure power before any other mujahedin could enter Laghman. He was voted into the Wolesi Jirga in 2005.

Agriculture, the main economic sector of Laghman, is irrigated through a series of canals and terraced fields from three rivers: the Alishing, Alingar, and Kabul. Most land only yields one crop per season, most of which is consumed by the farmers and their families or sold locally.

PHOTO BY MICHELLE PARKER

Chapter 4
The Economy

M ost of Laghman's population lives in a rural setting, making farming and herding the backbone of the economy. There are very few markets inside Laghman, so most produce must be transported to larger markets in Jalalabad and Kabul. Despite the importance of agriculture, more than one-third of households have employment income from non-farm sources such as laboring, mining, and timbering. Another third of households are engaged in trade and services. Many people work in Pakistan and Iran and send money back to their families. It is common for one income to support an entire extended family. The recent rise in food prices has been hard on people, as they grow many other crops that have not risen in value but still have to pay more for wheat and rice (the main staples). The economy has improved since the fall of the Taliban and development started, especially in places closer to Mehtarlam, with jobs increasing in urban areas for the government and military. However, the slow pace of development has been a complaint by most rural farmers, who expected much more development on a faster timeframe.

KEY SECTORS

Agriculture

The waters of the Alishing, Alingar, and Kabul Rivers feed an extensive series of irrigation canals and terraced fields. Various crops can be grown three times each year on irrigated land, and the most common are wheat, barley, rice, cotton, potatoes, cucumbers, beans, and squash. Rain-fed land generally yields only one crop each year, usually wheat. Most of these crops are consumed at home or sold in local markets. The lack of good transportation and market infrastructure makes marketing regionally or internationally very difficult. Unlike those in most other provinces, Laghmani farmers grow industrial crops if they store and transport well. Cotton, sugar, sesame, and olives are grown in both Mehtarlam and Qarghayi districts. The PRT and USAID are working with districts on large storage capabilities and value-added businesses such as canning and juicing to increase values.

Six percent of arable land is devoted to orchards. Stone fruits (apricots, peaches, and plums) are the most common, followed by citrus (oranges, lemons, and sweet oranges) and grapes. Persimmons, guava, pears, apples, and pomegranates are grown on a smaller scale. Walnuts, pine nuts, mulberries, and black persimmons are found in the province, mainly in the Alingar and Alishing valleys. USAID and several NGOs have extensive orchard assistance programs throughout the Eastern Region, including Laghman.

Livestock

Most farmers in the south keep two or three cows, while in the mountains of the north sheep and goats are more common. Almost all are used for personal consumption. Veterinary services are needed to keep this sector healthy, as the loss of only one animal is devastating to a family.

Trade and Industry

There are many small businesses in Laghman trading agricultural products and services, but, aside from an ice factory in Mehtarlam, there is no industry to speak of. Outside of the modest agricultural exports, smuggling stones and timber, and remittances from a sizable population of Laghmanis in Pakistan and Iran, there is no significant source of non-agricultural income.

Illegal Activities

A significant sector of the economy relies on the illegal trade of timber and gemstones, and a small group in the most remote areas relies on opium poppy cultivation. Timber and gemstone smuggling is being carried out by gangs of criminals in the valleys of Dawlat Shah, Alishing, and Alingar. Government officials are also involved in the smuggling industry, taking bribes to allow the trafficking to continue unchecked. The central government has banned all logging activity and requires special permits for hauling timber, but these regulations are largely not enforced. Poppy growth is minimal compared to Nangarhar or Helmand, but it remains a profitable alternative to growing legal crops in areas that are not under strict government control.

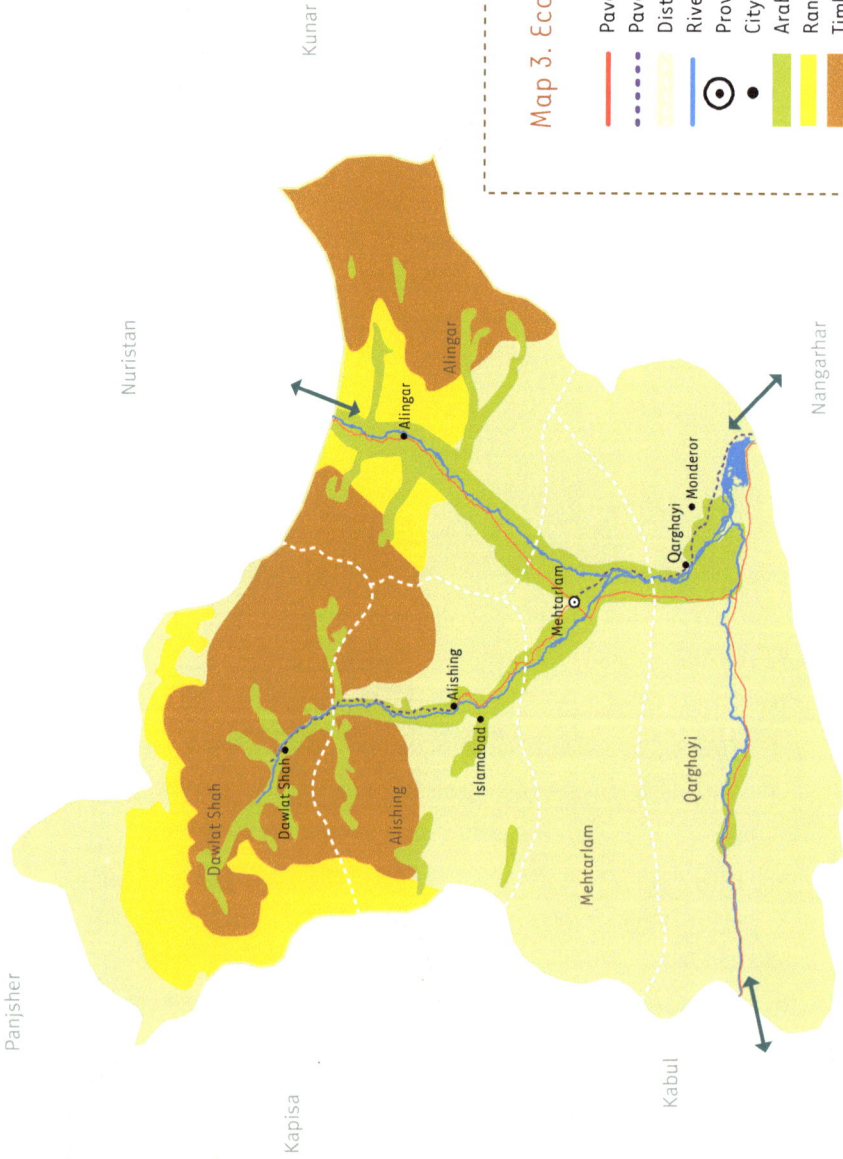

Map 3. Economic Map of Laghman

Paved Road
Paved Road (Planned)
District Border
River
Provincial Center
City
Arable Land
Range Land
Timber
Trade Routes

Panjsher

Kapisa

Nuristan

Kunar

Dawlat Shah

Alishing

Alishing

Islamabad

Alingar

Alingar

Mehtarlam

Mehtarlam

Qarghayi

Monderor

Qarghayi

Nangarhar

Kabul

TRENDS AND RELEVANT ISSUES FOR TODAY

Irrigation systems are a key part of Laghman's agriculture-based economy, but much of them have been destroyed or neglected after three decades of war. Repair and extension of the system could greatly increase farm output and raise living standards throughout the province. Several NGOs and government programs, such as NSP, are working on irrigation solutions, but these will take years of dedicated reconstruction to resolve. Increased production could allow Laghmanis to greatly expand their meager exports, but that will require the development of the food processing industry and more robust marketing cooperatives. USAID's Afghanistan Small and Medium Enterprise Development program (ASMED) is promoting the development of jams, honey, and other value-added programs to increase outputs and allow for better storage.

Flooding in April 2007 forced villagers from Qarghayi district to evacuate their homes. Massive flooding from rainfall and melting snow each year destroy the province's fragile intake system. The lack of watershed management and flood mitigation continues to be a challenge to reconstruction efforts in Laghman, with a majority of its population dependent on agriculture.

PHOTO BY AIR FORCE CAPT. GERARDO GONZALEZ

Chapter 5
International Organizations and
Reconstruction Activities

PROJECTS AND ACTIVITIES

Electricity

Laghman does not have a public power grid. Only 13 percent of households have access to electricity. Most of the power comes from micro-hydro plants or the diesel generators in downtown Mehtarlam. Outside of Mehtarlam, houses generally have only enough electricity to light a few rooms or power a television if the family wants to pay extra. Hydroelectric power has considerable potential along the rivers in the north, but it is not part of the Afghan government's national energy plan. Extensive potential for micro-hydro power exists in the province and, if tapped, could offset the large shortfall of power in the province. A recent study suggested that wind farms could be a reliable source of energy in Qarghayi. At this time it is not known how much power is possible or if that power would be used for Laghman or for nearby Jalalabad City, where there is a larger population.

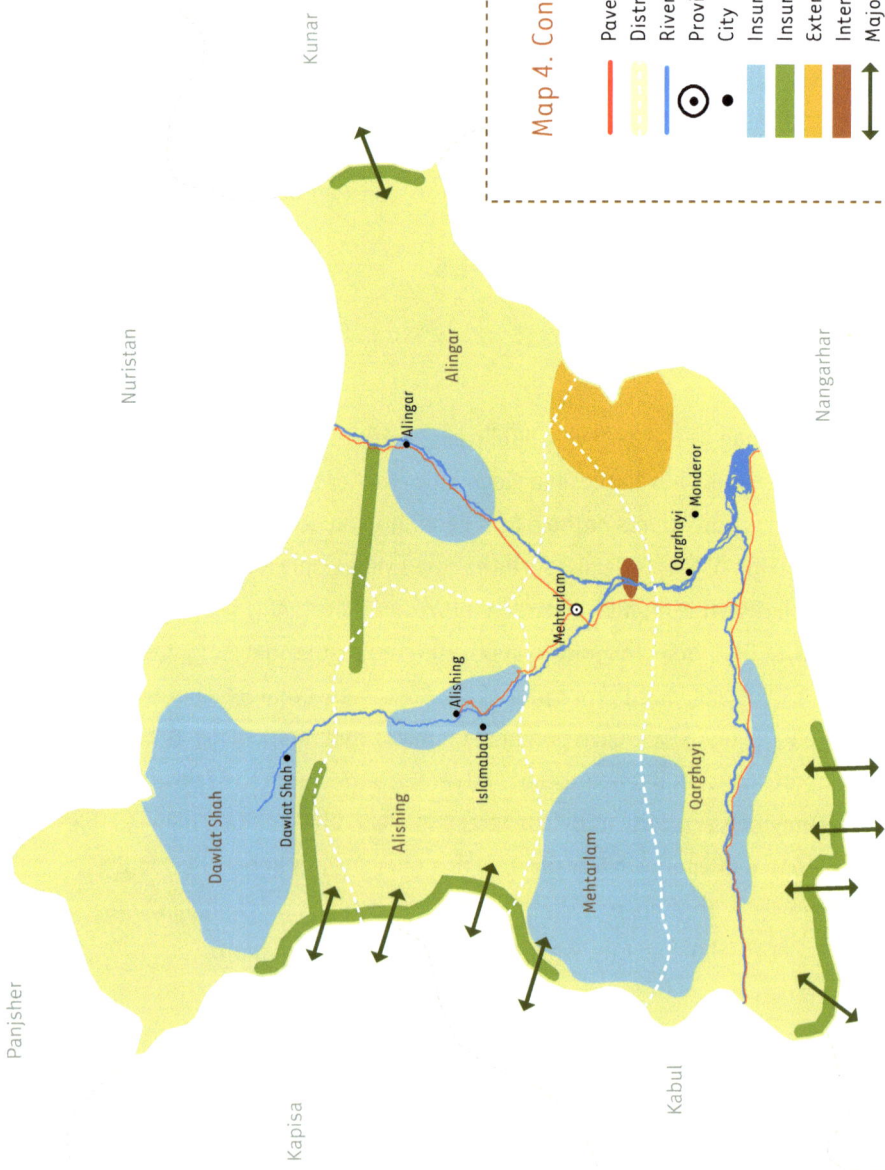

Map 4. Conflict Map of Laghman

Legend:
- Paved Road
- District Border
- River
- Provincial Center
- City
- Insurgent Activity Areas
- Insurgent Transit Areas
- External Tribal Conflict Areas
- Internal Tribal Conflict Areas
- Major Border Crossings

Provinces: Panjsher, Nuristan, Kunar, Nangarhar, Kabul, Kapisa

Districts and places: Alingar, Alingar, Mehtarlam, Monderor, Qarghayi, Qarghayi, Alishing, Alishing, Islamabad, Dawlat Shah, Dawlat Shah, Mehtarlam

Roads

Roads are essential for security, health, economic development, and communication, and will remain one of the top priorities in the near future. The main road from Mehtarlam to the Kabul-Jalalabad Highway was paved two years ago, and the main road from Mehtarlam through the eastern Alingar valley to Nuristan is now completely paved. The road from Mehtarlam through the western valley of Alishing and Dawlat Shah is under construction all the way to Nuristan. These two roads and the OP near Alishing have had a positive effect on both security and the economy along the Alishing branch. Plans to pave into some of the side valleys are underway. These road plans will link about 90 percent of the population in Laghman to the provincial capital, making transport of goods and services much more efficient while also extending the reach of the government into areas where it is relatively absent.

Irrigation

Reconstruction of destroyed irrigation systems has been slow in Laghman. Despite having three large rivers, the irrigation system is in such disrepair that the population only has access to a fraction of the water available to grow crops. Irrigation almost entirely relies on hundreds of individual intake systems from the rivers and streams. An intake is basically a wall built out into a river that funnels water into a canal system used to flood and irrigate fields. Unfortunately, massive floods destroy the intake systems every year when the mountain snow melts, forcing the population to rebuild their irrigation systems constantly. An extensive program which sets up sturdy intakes, watershed management, and flood mitigation is needed to break this cycle and ensure proper irrigation and thus agriculture systems in Laghman.

EDUCATION

Education is considered one of the main priorities for development in Laghman. About 142,000 students attend 157 primary and 78 secondary schools. Only 110 of these schools currently have buildings. Several donors have stepped in to build the remaining schools. There were 56 schools under construction in June 2009, leaving 69 schools without buildings. The need for classrooms is only increasing as more students attend school. The schools that were built only a few years ago are packed with children to the point where half the classes are held outside due to the lack of classroom space. A shortage of teachers and other resources also plagues the system, and assistance organizations need to coordinate closely to ensure that school buildings can be staffed and maintained. Boys are favored by their parents to attend school over girls, and they attend separate schools or at least are in separate classrooms. Although girls are allowed to attend primary school, few are able to attend high school.

Laghman also houses one religious school (*madrassa*) in each district. Madrassas are similar to the parochial school model in the US. They combine religious teaching with secular subjects. There are also religious schools called *darulhefazs* (one per district) where students only study the Koran.

Center of Education Excellence Construction

In 2007, Minister of Education Hanif Atmar announced a plan to construct 34 "super madrassas," or "Centers of Educational Excellence," throughout the country. The goal is to take back religious education from extremists in neighboring Pakistan and include secular education in the curriculum. The Mehtarlam PRT is funding the construction of the Laghman Center of Education Excellence, which will house 1,500-2,000 religious students. The facility includes dormitories, meeting rooms, and classrooms.

HEALTHCARE

The following types of health facilities are provided by the Ministry of Health:

Basic Health Center (BHC): Serves a population up to 30,000 people. Outpatient care only, similar to Level I military care. Basic OB/GYN, routine immunizations, childhood diseases, treatment of malaria, TB, and care for mental health patients and disabled patients.

Comprehensive Health Clinic (CHC): Serves a population up to 60,000 people. Similar to Level II military care. Limited inpatient care, basic laboratory, severe childhood illnesses, and malaria. Staffed with male and female doctors, nurses, midwives, lab, and pharmacy techs.

District/Provincial Level Hospitals provide the most comprehensive level of care.

Healthcare is a key issue in Laghman, especially in the districts furthest from Mehtarlam, which houses the only hospital in the province. Since 2001, the Afghan government has set up numerous basic health centers and comprehensive health centers with the support of donor organizations, but adequate healthcare remains one of the biggest complaints. Out of 620 villages, only 22 have a health center within their boundaries, 27 have a dispensary, and 44 have a drugstore.

Accessibility to healthcare is rather difficult for a large portion of the population, and just under two-thirds of residents (63.5 percent) have to travel over five km to get medical attention. Additionally, the poor road system makes it difficult for people to access basic care. The quality of care is still low if available at all. The majority of the population does not have a health worker permanently present in their community. Even moderately sick people often travel to Kabul or Pakistan to obtain better treatment.

PROVINCIAL RECONSTRUCTION TEAM

The PRT in Laghman consists of a military team and three US government civilian agencies. The military side consists of a Civil Affairs (CA) team, public affairs team, engineers, and support elements. The civilian side consists of representatives from the US Agency for International Development (USAID), US Department of State (DoS), and US Department of Agriculture (USDA). Laghman recently added an Agribusiness Development Team (ADT), consisting of National Guard soldiers with several agriculture specialists.

The PRT has taken a leading role in supporting development in the province and in working to build capacity at the district level. The military wing of the PRT has focused much of its attention on building the main paved road systems in the province and building schools in the province. USAID has begun a new $150 million five-year program in northern, eastern, and western Afghanistan called IDEA NEW to replace the completed Alternative Development Program. It is not known how much of this money will be used in Laghman, as plans are still under development. This program will focus on a range of projects including infrastructure, agriculture, gender activities, and business development. USAID also has the Local Governance and Community Development (LGCD) program, focused more on community-based projects and stability at the local governance level and, more specifically, in higher-risk areas of the province. The ADT will most likely focus its efforts on agriculture and irrigation issues, including watershed management and better farming methods.

NATIONAL SOLIDARITY PROGRAM

The National Solidarity Program (NSP) is a nationwide grassroots development program that places development in the hands of the local populations. Community Development Councils (CDCs) prioritize, plan, and implement local development projects such as irrigation systems and small electrical systems that benefit the whole community. This program is overseen by the directorate of Rural Rehabilitation and Development. This program has been vastly successful due to its grassroots empowerment of the local people. It has been marred by corruption and funding roadblocks at times but is considered one of the most successful development programs in Afghanistan.

Table 7. UN Organizations in Laghman

ACRONYM	FULL NAME	SECTORS
UNAMA	United Nations Assistance Mission in Afghanistan	Coordinates most UN/NGO activities
UNICEF	United Nations Children's Fund	Health, education, water and sanitation program (WATSAN), and child protection
UNHCR	United Nations High Commissioner for Refugees	Assists refugees and returnees
WFP	World Food Program	Rehabilitation programs include FOODAC, food-for-work, food-for-seeds and food-for training
UN-Habitat	United Nations Human Settlement Program	WATSAN, agriculture, and National Solidarity Program (NSP)

ACRONYM	FULL NAME	SECTORS
UNDP	United Nations Development Program	Supports/facilitates development through: 1. Afghan Information Management System (AIMS) 2. Urban Development Group (UDG) 3. National Area Based Development Program (NABDP)
WHO	World Health Organization	Assists in emergencies, controls communicable diseases, promotes public health and training
FAO	Food Agriculture Organization	Agricultural inputs, such as seeds, tools and emergency veterinary supplies/services
UNOPS	United Nations Office for Project Services	Implementing construction projects of USAID and other donors
UNODC	United Nations Office for Drug and Crimes	Strengthens government anti-narcotic agencies
UNMACA	United Nations Mine Awareness and Clearance Agency	De-mining unexploded ordnance in the region

Table 8. International NGOs in Laghman

ACRONYM	FULL NAME	MAIN ACTIVITIES
ACBAR	Agency Coordinating Body for Afghan Relief	Umbrella organization for NGOs in Afghanistan
AMI	Aide Medical International	Health
BRAC	Bangladesh Rural Advancement Committee	Microfinance
DACAAR	Danish Committee for Aid to Afghan Refugees	Water supply & sanitation
GAA/FSP	German Agro Action	Food security
ICARDA	International Center for Agricultural Research in the Dry Areas	Rehabilitation of agriculture and livestock, agriculture research
ICRC	International Committee of the Red Cross	Emergency relief for victims of armed conflicts
IF Hope	International Foundation of Hope	Agriculture, development, irrigation
IFRC	International Federation of Red Cross and Red Crescent Societies	Health, first aid, disaster preparedness

ACRONYM	FULL NAME	MAIN ACTIVITIES
IMC	International Medical Corps	Health
IOC	International Orphan Care	Vocational training and education for orphans
IRC	International Rescue Committee	Agriculture, education, small business assistance, engineering
MADERA	Mission d'Aide au Développement des Economies Rurales Programme Afghanistan	Agriculture, irrigation, microcredit and construction
NRC	Norwegian Refugees Council	Legal assistance, information education
RI	Relief International	Constructing clinics, schools, marketing centers, irrigation, micro credit
SCA	Swedish Committee for Afghanistan	Health, education, irrigation
SCS	Save the Children (Sweden/Norway)	Education

(Source: UNAMA)

Deputy Governor Murtaza Hedayt Qalandarzai speaks to RTA Laghman after engaging local village leaders. While radio is the most prevalent media in the province, television is the most watched in urban areas. Wealthier families have satellite dishes and enjoy Bollywood movie channels, Al Jazeera, CNN, and Fox News.

PHOTO BY SPC JASON DORSEY

Chapter 6
Information and Influence

In early 2009, the Taliban began an anti-coalition information operations (I/O) campaign in the otherwise pro-government area along the river south of Alingar. The Taliban has made intimidating threats, but since mid-2009, the population remains strongly pro-government.

TELECOMMUNICATIONS

There is no land-line telephone network in the province, but cellular service is widely available. All four of Afghanistan's wireless companies (Roshan, AWCC, Areeba, and Etesalat) are available in the capital. Roshan and AWCC have the larger coverage areas and are continually expanding throughout the province. There are no internet cafes in Laghman as of June 2009, but AWCC is offering internet access on its system via mobile phones, which works intermittently.

MEDIA

Laghman is a small province, so domestic and international media organizations do not maintain offices in Mehtarlam and instead cover the province from Jalalabad. There is a small association of local journalists in Laghman, but it is not very well organized. These journalists work for the government's radio and television stations, locally-run magazines, or the independent radio stations. Due to the high education rate in Laghman, many youth are interested in media activities and wish to become journalists.

Television

Television is mostly watched in the urban areas where generator power is shared among families, but some wealthier families in the outer districts run televisions off generators and satellite dishes. Indian television programs are also quite popular, with sports channels, "Bollywood" movie channels, and news channels. Indian culture seems intrigue most young Afghans. There are also religious channels such as "Peace TV" from India that preach moderate Islam, and American and other foreign news channels such as Al Jazeera, CNN, and Fox News, creating a truly balanced media.

Radio

Radio is the most common media outlet used in the province. Over the past four years, thousands of radios have been handed out by US troops, and most people have access to one now. Many radio stations from Nangarhar now reach into Laghman, providing more variety. Major radio stations play music, host call-in shows, and spread the daily news. Although the government has its own radio station, RTA, private stations are the favorites of the youth who were starved for music and media during the Taliban regime.

Print

Newspapers and magazines are less prevalent in the outer areas where literacy is low, but they are snatched up quickly when soldiers hand them out in villages. Several people begin reading them immediately but others will take several papers and run back home. It is not known how many are read.

Table 9. Television Stations

NAME	MANAGER/ OWNER	GOVERNMENT OR PRIVATE	BROADCAST HOURS	PHONE
RTA– Laghman	Muhebollah	Government	1200 – 2200	0700-161-885

Table 10. Radio Stations

NAME	FREQUENCY/ BAND	MANAGER/ OWNER	GOVERNMENT OR PRIVATE	PHONE
RTA – Laghman	97.3 FM	Mohebullah	Government	0700-161-885
Radio Caun Voice	88.5 FM	Unknown	Private	Unknown
Radio Kawoon	90.0 FM	Zwan Enqelabi	Private	0799-619-092

Broadcasting a wide range of programming, from music to call-in talk shows, radio has quickly become the most popular media in Laghman. While the government owns RTA Laghman, private radio stations have made the biggest impact, attracting a younger audience that was starved for music during the Taliban regime.

PHOTO BY CAPT BERNICE LOGAN

Table 11. Print Media Sources

NAME	FREQUENCY	MANAGER/ OWNER	GOVERNMENT OR PRIVATE	PHONE
Zarkamar Magazine	Timely	Zwan Enqelabi	Private	0799-619-092
Roshan Magazine	Timely	Mohamad Sarwar	Private	0707-788-751

INFORMATION SHARING NETWORKS

Informal channels are the most common method of spreading information and influencing the population outside of major towns. Mosques are one of the most influential ways information is spread. Prayer times at mosques, especially Friday prayers, are the times when everyone is together, gossiping and talking about recent events. The fast spread of mobile phones has sped up the information sharing networks. It seems that nearly everyone has a mobile phone. Often a village that does not know a military convoy is coming will be ready when it arrives because someone saw it on the way and phoned ahead.

Many landowners have a small congregation area where local villagers meet to talk about the day's events, listen to radios, and gossip. In any village, there will be men sitting around talking in small groups. Older men constantly talk about politics and corruption in the government and economic problems. It seems that each of them has a conspiracy theory about the government and international community. Younger men talk more about education and finding a job. The youth are much more impressionable. Children that only five years ago hardly spoke and seemed oblivious to what is happening around them are now becoming young men with staunch opinions, hungry for change and prosperity.

Laghman's chief of police, General Omaryar, conducts a village assessment with a Civil Affairs team. Across the country, people see the Afghan National Police (ANP) as corrupt and unreliable.

PHOTO BY ARMY SPC HENRY SELZER 173RD AIRB

Chapter 7
Big Issues

AFGHAN NATIONAL SECURITY FORCES

The Afghan National Police are the key to stability in Laghman. They number about 700. As of early 2007, the Afghan National Army presence was limited to about 60-80 soldiers at the base in Mehtarlam and about 30 soldiers at Security Base Najil at the juncture of the Mayl and Alishing valleys, 26 km to the north. Police reform has been underway for sometime now, but it has a long way to go. The police have been severely underpaid and are seen by much of the local population as thieves and thugs who accept bribes, extort money, and flat-out steal from the people they are supposed to protect. The provincial police chiefs in Laghman from 2004 to 2006 were extremely corrupt and allegedly involved in drug trafficking. The arrival of General Abdul Kareem Omaryar in October of 2006 brought some significant improvements. General Omaryar has received good reviews for his first 18 months in the province. He has been a vocal supporter of both the central and provincial governments and a leader in poppy eradication.

Mentoring the ANP on professionalism and behavior is paying dividends. They are earning the trust of the population and becoming an effective information-gathering and law enforcement force capable of establishing and maintaining security and stability. Past unreliability of the ANP created great tension with ANA forces in the province, which resulted in shootouts between the two groups. The ANP looks to OEF/ISAF for examples of professional behavior. With encouragement and cooperation from its leaders, the ANA could serve as an example as well. Until the ANP gains the trust of the population and begins to receive information from them on bombings, weapon caches, and insurgent and criminal activity, stability and security will be tenuous at best.

INTERNAL CONFLICTS: MUJAHEDIN PARTIES

The rivalries between former mujahedin strongmen are still factors in Laghman today, so it is important to understand the history and where people's allegiances lie. Laghman remains a competition ground for the two big parties, HIG and JI. Jamiat's Dr. Abdullah has supporters in central and western Mehtarlam and Qarghayi as well as through the provincial NDS network.

It is important to understand that all rivals may try to harm their enemies by giving false information to coalition forces. Therefore, information may not be reliable, even if it is from a government official. It is strongly recommended that reports of government corruption or criminal activity, especially against newly-appointed officials, be treated skeptically until personal, tribal, and power motivations can be identified and understood.

WEAPONS AND DRUGS SMUGGLING

Laghman borders three unstable provinces, Nuristan, Kunar, and Kapisa, and a major poppy producing province, Nangarhar. Its valleys and passes are commonly used as smuggling routes by weapons and drugs smugglers alike. For example, the northern portion of Alingar is a favorite thorough-fare for the movement of funds and weapons from eastern Afghanistan. As for drugs, Nangarhar was the hub of opium refining for most of eastern Afghanistan for years. Poppy would come from Badakhshan and Takar through Laghman, get processed into opium in Nangarhar, and return north, where it would be exported through the Central Asian republics. Although the north has set up its own refineries, Nangarhar continues to receive a steady flow of customers from the north.

DEVELOPMENT SURGE

After seven years of international military and civilian presence in Laghman, the local population is frustrated with the slow pace of development. Expectations will be raised even further by the news that the United States intends to put more resources into Afghanistan. Meeting those expectations will determine whether or not the coalition is successful in building an effective government that has the support of the population.

Some of these new resources will allow the coalition to increase and expand existing programs. A consensus has emerged in the past few years that roads need to be a priority because they are basic to the economy and security. Similarly, improving water availability and irrigation systems in a province that relies overwhelmingly on agriculture will undoubtedly resonate with the vast majority of the population.

The surge also will present unique challenges. While more troops will provide more security for projects, allow the training of more ANSF, and give the insurgents fewer places to hide, they will also be an irritant to those who resent a foreign presence in their country. Troops will need to be increasingly careful to keep a lower profile and keep the ANA and ANP out front. Enhanced information operations (I/O) to promote the coalition's good deeds and to manage consequences of the inevitable missteps will be necessary.

Most children in Laghman are sent to school in the mornings. Some boys wake early to take the family's cows to the fields. After school, boys head to the mosque to study the Holy Koran with the Imam, while girls stay home and assist their mother in preparing the next meal.

PHOTO BY CAPT WALTER CHRISTIAN

Appendices

TIMELINE OF KEY EVENTS

February 2005: USAID begins a five-year, $150 million Alternative Development Program to bring major economic development to the Eastern Region.

Fall 2006: A major road system is paved, linking Kabul, Jalalabad, and Mehtarlam. The roads improve trade and boost Laghman's economy.

Spring 2007: Major floods cause hundreds of deaths and massive damage to agricultural land in the Alingar and Alishing river basins.

Summer 2007: Member of Parliament Esmatullah Mohabat is assassinated. The motive is rumored to be a personal dispute.

Summer 2007: The PRT begins an ongoing plan to pave all major roads in the province. This program will increase market accessibility and allow for government influence in areas that are currently neglected.

March 2008: Lutfullah Mangal becomes governor of Laghman.

January 2009: US forces attack insurgents in Masamut-e Bala and Galouch villages, where several civilians are reportedly killed in the fighting, creating animosity towards the US military.

May 2009: Mayor of Mehtarlam, Mohammad Rahim, is assassinated. Motive is unknown.

COMMON COMPLIMENTS REGARDING THE US MILITARY IN THE EASTERN REGION

- Afghans compliment the US forces' work ethic and say it drives them to work harder for themselves.

- Afghans are happy when projects change their lives for the better after decades of war, such as road construction. In Laghman, the roads linking Mehtarlam to Alishing and Alingar are particularly appreciated.

- Afghans appreciate the medical and education assistance provided by the soldiers.

- Afghans respect the US soldiers for leaving their families to come and help them.

- Afghans are especially moved by the deaths of US soldiers. In Laghman, Sgt 1st Class Meredith Howard from the PRT was killed by an IED, and the population was extremely saddened by the tragedy.

COMMON COMPLAINTS REGARDING THE US MILITARY IN THE EASTERN REGION

- Afghans claim that US forces have inflicted excessive civilian casualties while taking out few insurgent leaders.

- Afghans complain that the US forces raid their houses at night without cause or government support.

- Afghans believe Americans use informers for their intelligence gathering who are not being honest. Most of these people have their own agendas and manipulate the truth.

- Afghans lament that ISAF and other foreign personnel do not know or understand the local people and what is going on among them. They don't always respect the religion or culture because they do not understand.

- Afghans complain when US forces drive them off the roads carelessly or block a road for hours without letting even sick or injured people to pass.

DAY IN THE LIFE OF A RURAL LAGHMANI

The life of a rural Laghmani starts very early in the morning with the imam's call to prayer one hour before sunrise. Men of the family get up, wash, and go to their village mosque for the first prayer of the day. The young boys take the cows to the fields. Women pray at home, start a fire, and prepare breakfast. Breakfast in the house of a poor man is just sweet green tea and bread, and a wealthier man will have milk, cheese, and home made butter. After breakfast, men go to the field and women stay behind at home or go help their men in the field. In the mountainous valleys, Pashai men take animals a long distance to graze, and women work on the fields and collect wood for the family. Children go to school to study.

Usually everyone returns home for lunch at midday, but sometimes men will stay in the field. A typical lunch for Laghmanis is rice and cereal with cooked vegetables, and is always accompanied with yogurt and slices of onion or other kinds of fresh vegetables from the fields.

After lunch, everyone prays in the afternoon and then takes a nap. When they wake up, they have green tea and work again in the field. Next is the third prayer of the day, when men gather in front of mosques or under the shade of a tree and catch up on the happenings from the day before. Children go to the mosque to study the Holy Koran and other religious books with the imam. Women milk the animals and process cheese, butter, and yogurt in the cool of the late afternoon.

The fourth prayer of the day takes place before dinner, and when it is complete, everyone rushes home to eat dinner as a family. After dinner the family talks about the day's events and discusses the plan for the next day. Then the final prayer of the day is completed and everyone goes to sleep. During the summer, Laghmanis sleep outside on their roofs.

FURTHER READING AND SOURCES

Books

- Louis Dupree, *Afghanistan*, Princeton: Princeton University Press, 1979.

- *ISAF PRT Handbook*, 3rd Ed., February 2007, NATO.

- Edward Girardet and Jonathan Walter, Afghanistan: *Essential Field Guides to Humanitarian and Conflict Zones,* CROSSLINES Publication Ltd., 1998 and 2004, *www.crosslinesguides.com.*

- Ahmed Rashid, *Taliban: Militant Islam, Oil and Fundamentalism in Central Asia*, 2001.

- Ahmed Rashid, *Descent into Chaos: The United States and the Future of Nation Building in Afghanistan, Pakistan, and Central Asia*, Viking Press, 2008.

- Larry Goodson, *Afghanistan's Endless War: State Failure, Regional Politics, and the Rise of the Taliban*, 2001.

- Greg Mortenson, *Three Cups of Tea: One Man's Mission to Promote Peace... One School at a Time*, 2007. (excellent understanding of how to succeed with the people and culture)

- Barnett Rubin, 1) *The Fragmentation of Afghanistan*, and 2) *Afghanistan's Uncertain Transition from Turmoil to Normalcy*, 2001 and 2007.

- Michael Griffin, *Reaping the Whirlwind: The Taliban Movement in Afghanistan*, London: Pluto Press, 2001.

- Steve Coll, *Ghost Wars: The Secret History of the CIA, Afghanistan, and Bin Laden, From the Soviet Invasion to September 10, 2001*, New York Penguin Press, 2004.

- Ben Macintyre, *The Man Who Would Be King: The First American in Afghanistan*, New York: Farrar, Straus and Giroux, 2005.

Articles

- "The Afghanistan National Development Strategy," President Karzai, 2006, *www.reliefweb.int/rw/RWFiles2006.nsf/ FilesByRWDocUNIDFileName/KHII-6LK3R2-unama-afg-30jan2. pdf/$File/unama-afg-30jan2.pdf*

- "Elections in 2009 and 2010: Technical and Contextual Challenges to Building Democracy in Afghanistan, Afghanistan Research and Evaluation Unit," November 2008, *www.areu.org. af/index.php?option=com_docman&Itemid=26&task=doc_ download&gid=612 -*

- "Potential Analysis of the Eastern Region and Nangarhar Province and Implication in Programming," Raphy Favre. *www.aizon.org/ Nangarhar%2oPotential%2oAnalysis.pdf*

Web Sites

- Afghanistan Research and Evaluation Unit (publishes the Afghanistan A to Z guide), *www.areu.org.af/index. php?option=com_frontpage&Itemid=25*

- Afghanistan Information Management Services, *www.aims.org.af*

- Afghanistan Online (Links to Official IRA and embassy websites), *www.afghan-web.com/politics*

- Naval Postgraduate School Program for Culture and Conflict Studies, *www.nps.edu/Programs/CCS/index.html*

- USAID, *www.usaid.gov/locations/asia/countries/afghanistan*

www.ingramcontent.com/pod-product-compliance
Lightning Source LLC
Chambersburg PA
CBHW040128270326
41927CB00001B/29